FINANCES

ARE LINKED

TO

EMOTIONS

Live Within Your Means

Bahiyah Shabazz

authorHOUSE®

AuthorHouse™
1663 Liberty Drive, Suite 200
Bloomington, IN 47403
www.authorhouse.com
Phone: 1-800-839-8640

First published by AuthorHouse 3/6/2009

ISBN: 978-1-4389-5565-0 (sc)

Printed in the United States of America
Bloomington, Indiana

This book is printed on acid-free paper.

Table of Contents

1. Introduction 1

2. Taking Care of Oneself 7
   A. Individual Therapy 8
   B. Couple Therapy 15
   C. Educational Therapy 22
   D. Personal Management 27
   E. Self Reliance 30
   F. Emotional Spending 41
   G. Emergency Fund 43

3. Financial Education 47
   A. Establishing & Maintaining Credit 48
   B. Deposit Accounts 59
   C. Budget & Managing 62

4. Letters of Concern 69

5. Belief in Success 79

****

Introduction

****

In 2008, President Bush disbursed an economic stimulus check to do just as Congress and he wanted…to stimulate the economy. The main purpose of the funds was to get the economy out of a spiral recession with hopes of migrating away from potential depression. This wasn't the first time an economic stimulus check was disbursed. As I recall everyone who qualified received one in 2001. The goal was achieved and most individuals put the funds from the check back into the economy just as the administration calculated. Depression, sadness, fear, joy, happiness, and excitement are feelings that are linked to finances. I believe once we obtain and understand the education of finance along with taking care of oneself our dollars will go much further than expected. Let's take an economic stimulus check of $1200 for a married couple.

The monies can be spent in numerous ways such as vacationing, purchase of a leather sofa, or a well deserved shopping spree. Too many people young, old, single, married, with or without children are spending money they don't have on frivolous items. Once we understand the process of emotional spending that same $1200 can be invested and work much harder for the same married couple instead of having nothing to show for a boost in income that is unaccountable.

Ex: Married Couple 35 yrs of age
Retirement age: 65 yrs old
Years spend in retirement: 20 yrs
Money set aside for retirement: $1200
Aggressive % for investing: 11% *
Moderate % during retirement: 7% *

The couple would need $1,003,585 by the time of retirement. The $1200 would accumulate to **$27,471** in 30years if invested. What a difference...

*Hypothetical interest and calculation

I have personally gone shopping with a group
of friends to hear most of them complain
about not having any money, but the desire to
purchase a trinket or two. There was a situation
when a good friend and I were shopping at
a renowned, "bringing the stars together"
store. She didn't have enough to meet her
means. The utilities were in shot off status; the
plumbing was horrible and couldn't properly
flush the toilet, and food was a commodity,
but shopping wasn't a leisure activity in her
mind. She indicated the extra money could go
toward the household, but she couldn't help but
spend her money on the repeated silk shirts.
Anita claimed how great she felt when making
spontaneous purchases. Her famous phrase
was "sometimes you got to treat yourself".
The problem was she *always* treated herself.

The circle of friends hated to tell her of planned shopping sprees because we knew what to expect. She would invite herself and no one would reject or say the wiser of her actions. I knew and believed my good friend was affected by emotional spending. In spite of her dilemmas, she spends extra monies on frivolous items to make herself feel good and avoid the unfortunate choices she continuously makes. To my dismay, she isn't the *only* one making negative choices and victimizing oneself of emotional spending.

****

Taking
Care
Of
Oneself

****

Individual Therapy

*I am almost positive that everyone knows
someone who tries to keep up with the Jones.
Let's look at Jennifer who clearly lives outside
her means. On the outside, she has a beautiful
home, new Mercedes Benz, and a wardrobe to
match her attitude. She makes an annual income
of $95,000.00. However, her disposable income
is limited and an emergency fund consists of
a phone call to her parents for another loan
that would never be paid back. No one knows
her struggles of portraying to others a woman
of statute with expensive jewelry, large square
footage home, and a foreign vehicle equipped
with everything. As previously mentioned
she asks her parents for small loans that are
withdrawn from their retirement fund.*

She is also no stranger to credit cards.
Although most are maxed out, she manages
to open more to live the lifestyle she portrays.
Jennifer has come to a point in her life that she
can't suffer any longer. She admits her debt
excluding mortgage comes to $300,000.00.
Her credit cards used from purchasing food
to exotic trips to Africa and Europe.

Jennifer clearly has a problem with debt. Her dilemma with finances and having a sense to want to belong started as far back as her teen years. I asked Jennifer as far back she could remember to describe an incident trying to keep up with someone outside her means. She smiled and stated, "high school". High school is a time when most of us are confused about where we should belong. There are groups from popular, jocks, nerds, outcasts, etc. Jennifer wanted to be a popular girl, but didn't initially look the part. She recalls begging her parents to shop at the designer stores and paying for spring break trips.

I decided to have Jennifer start with taking care of herself, realizing who she truly is, accept it, and then tackle her debt. She was hesitant because she presented a façade for so long. Everyone who knew her categorized her as the "it" girl. No one realized the pain and loneliness she had. Jennifer let the materials define who she was when in fact she was a carefree woman with goals and ambitions. Her goal was to actually love herself and enjoy life as well as defining her level of success. While having the discussion with me she admittedly cried about dying with debt and having nothing worthwhile to show for all her hard work.

Steps needing to take in order
to address the issues:

1. Admit to identifying one based
    on others' perception.

2. Define who *you* are and embrace it.

3. Identify all your debt to
    begin elimination.

4. Start eliminating the high
    interest credit cards first.

5. Decide what could be eliminated
    from a daily routine and put the
    cash away in an emergency fund.

Jennifer slowly began to attend to the issues.
She was not sure how long the debt elimination
was going to take, but was anxious to try.
Jennifer phoned all the credit card companies
to ask for a reduction in interest rate. With a
little negotiation, all of them granted her the
request. Every time she paid off one credit card
that dollar amount in addition to the current
payment was applied toward the bill. Because
Jennifer was determined and focused, she
never had to call her parents to bail her out of a
financial crisis. It seemed that her financial crisis
was due to a handbag, shoes, or suit on sale.

The more debt she paid off the better she
began to feel about herself. While meeting
with Jennifer during a follow up appointment,
I noticed an assertiveness and pride about
herself. It seemed the clothes, material
possessions no longer defined her, but her sense
of awareness, and self-love exuded confidence.

Couple Therapy

John and Mary is an average couple. She is an elementary school teacher and he is a self-employed contractor. They have two children, Eloise and Bethany ages 12years and 8years. Mary loves being an educator as well as the flexibility of being home with the girls during summer and holiday breaks. However, she misses her husband because he works long hours. He's a great contractor and is in full demand, which is great for business. She plans the family vacations and outings and tells him when and where to attend.

For doing so, Mary rewards herself with shopping sprees and spa treatments. They have shared accounts, but separate credit cards. One day John came home and noticed the mail on the end table. He looked at the return address and noticed the credit card company. He opened the mail and noticed the amount. He initially began to call the company because he thought it was a mistake. As he picked up the phone, he noticed the name on the account was his wife. He was astonished to see she charged up $25000.00 on one credit card. His heart sunk deep into his chest, as he felt betrayed and deceived.

John and Mary sat in the office in complete silence. John was clearly upset with his wife. She on the other hand believed she did nothing wrong since the card is in her name. John threw the bill on the desk and asked about the steps to eradicate the debt. He was financially prudent. They established 12 months of salary in an emergency fund, variable annuity, mutual funds, bonds, and 529 plans. I started by asking him how he felt about the situation. He indicated, "BETRAYED, DECEIVED, LIED TO". Mary was shocked to hear the words considering she believed to disclose everything she felt he should know.

The feelings he described were emotions
of infidelity. She in fact was disloyal about
the finances. Mary needed to recognize
her mistake and address the issue at hand.
Mary used her loneliness as an excuse to
splurge and treat herself. She never regarded
his feelings or thought about how this act
would possibly devastate him. John worked
long hours to provide for his f amily.

The last thing he wanted to feel was a lack of
control on his household. He looked for his
wife to be his partner and discuss everything
that happened in the household. Marriage is the
combining of two individuals working as one.

Steps needing to take in order
to address the issues:

1. Keep lines of communication open.

2. Incorporate date nights outside
   of family outings.

3. Discover an inexpensive hobby to
   alleviate sense of loneliness.

4. Pay off the credit card balance.

5. Reevaluate financial and retirement goals.

After creating a list of issues to address, the
communication opened. Mary realized she
disclosed limited information. They both made
time to converse with each other, which changed
the spending behavior. When Mary began
to feel acknowledged, she no longer needed
the shopping spree and spa treatments. John
began to be more involved in the household
finances, hence more involvement in the
business bookkeeping. I recommended they
pay off the credit card debt. I truly believed
this was an unselfish act. This was Mary's
first time running up the credit card balance.
They saved $175000 in an emergency fund.
The savings account is drawing 4.75%,
while the credit rate is 15.25% APR.

The interest earned on the savings accounts
is far less than the interest applied toward the
credit card debt. It makes sense to pay off the
credit card debt with the savings, eradicate the
credit balance, and replenish the emergency
fund. The two continue to meet for follow up
appointments and well as address any issues that
could possibly affect the financial household.

Numerous couples are affected by lack of
communication. This behavior plagues
companionship, well being, and finances.
Once you create financial infidelity, it
becomes hard to rely on the other person
for financial comfort. As with anything
else, with hard work you can prevail.

Educational Therapy

Bryson Smith is a bright, intelligent, young man. He recently graduated from High School to begin college in the fall. His parents thought it would be a good idea for him to meet with me so that I could educate him about finances. They were late bloomers in the department; therefore, they were not too sure how to inform him on the proper steps to take for financial freedom. We began the appointment by discussing his passions, goals, and future. He loves to read, write poetry, and play sports. He would love to travel the world and become an anthropologist. Since he was starting out in the real world, I thought it would be appropriate to discuss deposit accounts and credit.

I could have been speaking a different language because he had no idea what I was indicating. Deposit accounts are checking, savings, and certificate of deposits. These accounts assist to function financially. It establishes a financial relationship with banks and credit unions. The accounts will also pay the person interest for "parking" the monies while the institutions uses the funds for its convenience. Since you are going to college, everyone is going to offer and possibly approve a credit card. Credit cards can help with establishing credit if used, as it should be.

Students or anyone establishing a financial relationship for the first time can be overwhelmed. However, if used properly it can work to anyone's advantage.

Steps needing to take in order to address the issues:

1. Open deposit accounts to establish
    a financial relationship.

2. Balance check book.

3. Apply for one credit card.

4. Budget and manage funds while in school.

5. Have a part time job and begin an IRA.

Bryson's parents decided to take him to the
local bank and open a college checking account
and apply for a student credit card. He was
approved and all were excited. The information
was brought by and shared. I encouraged
Bryson to use the credit card to his advantage.
Many people believe a credit card is the start
to bad credit. I beg to differ. A responsible
individual can use a credit card to help establish
and build positive credit. The key is to pay at
least the minimum balance monthly and not
to use more than fifty-five percent. Since he
was part of a work-study program, it wouldn't
be difficult for him to pay off small balances
on the credit card. Begin by setting up direct
deposit so that all the conveniences of a
deposit account are taking advantage. Next,
open an IRA to start the retirement goals.

Since he is starting at a young age time, volatility and patience is on his side. The younger an individual starts a retirement account the better chances he or she has with reaching the financial goals much sooner as well as having time in favor. College students are new comers to the financial world. It is imperative to educate the youth in all facets of life. Bryson and his parents were pleased with the advice taken away from the meetings and applied to his life. He continues to revisit when he's home during breaks. Since he has been responsible with his established credit he feels good about himself. Bryson also periodically checks his credit report and is pleased with the positive credit score that is reflecting his level of responsibility.

I am pleased to say that Bryson is on his way to being a responsible young man. He clearly has parents whom are supportive and willing to contribute to his success.

Personal Management

Think about a time when your finances were
affected by your emotions. Did you shop due
to depression? Elation? Sorrow? Neglect?
Boredom? It's time to address the concerns
that can permanently affect your well-being.
Too many times, I hear individuals state that
their lives would be different if they had more
money. That's not necessarily true. Individuals
can be financially rich along with emotional
neglect. The combination of the two is a recipe
for continuous (negative) behavior. In order
to eradicate the spending habits and lack of
financial concerns one must discuss the emotions
and behaviors that lead toward self -destruction.

List three emotions that lead *you* to impulsive spending:

1.

2.

3.

How did you feel afterwards? Were you ambivalent about your purchases? Did you justify your spending?

It's time to identify the source to your emotional spending. In order for each household to move forward with goals rather, it's financially, career, and family one must have a plan. A plan to list what has to be accomplished. Discuss how to reach each goal and identify the emotional state of the key holders in the plan.

It's time to discuss personal management. Each person no matter the socioeconomic class should identify what the meanings of finances are and take a deeper look at their emotions. Emotions are stronger than we realize. It allows us to make pertinent decisions that can ultimately affect lives.

Self Reliance

Why do I define myself by the material items I possess and not by who I am?

Many can identify with living by other
standards and not your own. Realizing
and accepting who you are is critical to
addressing your issues. I don't want to blame
one industry or individual, but television
plays an intricate role in shaping society.
Commercials and sitcoms are captivating
and filled with subliminal endorsements.
It's the who's who of what to emulate.

Once it is realized that a small percentage live by
an elite standard the better people will become.
Many believe that in order to be accepted
you have to look a certain way. However, the
acceptance should begin with self. Again, once
you accept yourself then others will follow.

Disclosing who you truly are is frightening,
but can also be liberating. I have learned
that each person have four sides.

Who you present to others	Who you conceal from others
Who you are learning	Who you don't know yourself

Each part makes a person whole. Looking
at the chart clearly identifies the lack
of self-reliance many have that leads to
irrational spending habits. The two top
boxes weigh heavily on an individual.

Defining yourself by the material possessions
is concealment of oneself. *What are
you afraid to present to others?*

During childhood, we are free persons
without a care in the world. Everything
is playful, innocent, and pure. Something
happens as we mature; something
shapes our minds about ourselves.

I once sat with a client who could vividly
remember her first thoughts as a toddler. As
impressing as it was the memories were also
confirmation of an early independence.

Marissa recalls at the age of three learning to
roller skate. Her father purchased the Fisher
Price adjustable beginner skates. She would
put the skates on daily to learn how to fall and
try again. She was teased by the neighborhood
kids. Because not only she continuously fell, but
also the skates were adjustable with huge Velcro
straps. Marissa didn't care as she remembers
proudly wearing the plastic skates and learning
how to skate. Her father told her she was
beautiful. He understood her independence. She
knew to continue to dust herself off whenever
she fell. At the age of three, she presented an
independent little person who accepted who she
was and proudly displayed her tenacity to others.

Marissa eventually matured, but her expectations
of herself did not. She along with others
presents what she believes to be the epitome
of a round individual. Somewhere between
the independent toddler and the mature adult
self-reliance was lost. She layers her clothing
just as she layers her emotions. Each piece
is a sum of the parts that makes us whole.

Will anyone truly know or even understand why
a person defines oneself by material items? I
believe so. However, the answer is customized
to the individual. Addressing what is sought
after when emotionally spending and shopping
can become clear when discussing defining
oneself by items and not by your self worth.

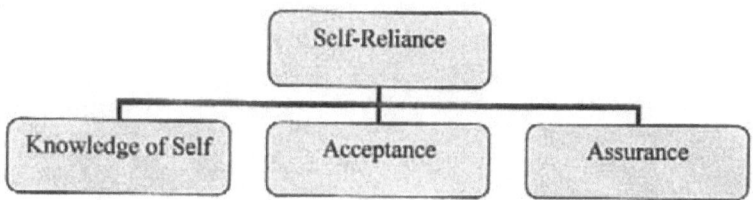

Again, there is Anita who likes to spend and lives by the motto "sometimes you got to treat yourself". One day I privately met with Anita to discuss her thought process about finances.

She arrived early to the appointment draped in Chanel and fierce Jimmy Choo shoes. Her attire was a layout from the photos of Vanity Fair. She looked and carried herself like a million bucks. However, her deposit accounts screamed something different.

I began by asking why she chose shopping
as a priority. Anita explained she felt as
good as she looked. Although she had the
worst circumstances, couldn't get ends to
meet and wore outfits that cost more than a
semester's tuition she felt great. She learned
to measure her successes by the material
items she wore. Anita disclosed people
were able to see her attire and vehicles and
not her retirement or emergency funds.

The first step to address with Anita is the lack
of taking care of oneself (self-reliance). Anita
must begin by taking off the layers of clothing
she shields herself with the designer suits. True
respect is self-respect. Learn to love who are
and what you represent and others will follow.

I agreed with her that no one sees what she has established in an emergency fund or retirement plan, but that should be the least of her concerns. Knowing and accepting who you are is preservation of the soul. She is a prime candidate of lack of self-reliance, emotional spending, and lack of budgeting.

Anita is like many others that thrive on perceptions outside of her thought process. I challenged her to address who she is without the clothing. That entails stripping down to her emotional nakedness and become vulnerable. Look deep within to discover why she wants to "look good" for others.

After involvement with many consultations, I have come to notice that individuals fall into one of three categories:

1. Keeping up with the Jones

People live outside their means and adopt the "by any means necessary" attitude. They value material items more than retirement plans, individual stocks and real estate. Most lack self control of their spending habits and thrive on looking like the "it" woman or man. They would do anything to be the center of attention and long for others to want to emulate their style.

2. A means to no end

These individuals work to spend money. Their paychecks are recklessly depleted on items *but* the monthly bills are barely met. Most realize they have a predicament with emotional spending. However, they desire to live outside the household budget. Once spending is realized and controlled, they have the opportunity to save, budget, and manage finances.

3. Limited functional well being

They are contemplating bankruptcy as a way out of their dilemma. They have splurged on items with credit and loans. They display lack of financial education about what it means to establish and maintain good credit. Unfortunately, they don't have the desire to *keep up with the Jones*. Instead, they are attempting to keep up with the minimum to survive from the collection calls. Having lack of funds is indicative of displaying poor money management skills. Bankruptcy seems to be the only way out. However, with firm discipline, negotiation and consultation there is a light at the end of the tunnel.

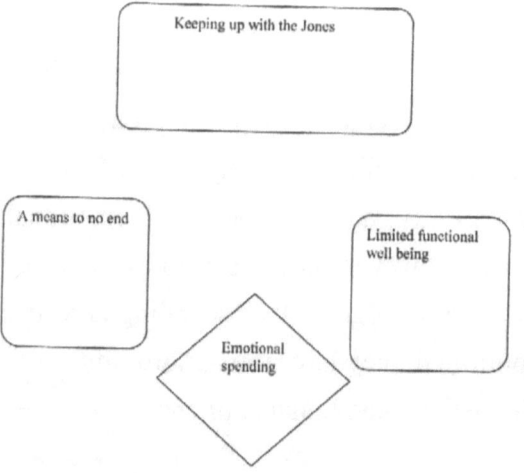

Emotional Spending

Why do I live paycheck to paycheck to feel good about myself?

I have discovered that too many of us are driven by our emotions. This isn't necessarily a bad thing, but it can lead to discomfort. Emotions are intense feelings that coerce a decision from individuals. To a person's surprise, the outcome may not deliver the results expected from the intentions. Couples question their marriage, individuals wonder about well-being. In order to address any underlying issues we must discuss what leads a person to spend out of control and live for others. Let's look at Chloe. I'm sure everyone knows a "Chloe". This person only cares about how she looks no matter the situation. Everyone isn't this extreme, but the circumstance is familiar.

I have spoken with numerous persons valuing
themselves by the designer material items
owned so that they can portray to others a
well presented person. "Treating yourself"
as people like to call it should not only imply
splurging on clothing. It should consist of
putting money away for an emergency fund,
a rainy day or retirement. Once we accept
the importance of self we can understand
"treating yourself" *can* also mean taking
care of you. As always, people ask the mind
puzzling questions about reasons for actions.

Emergency Fund

Will I have enough money put away if I lose my job?

Heidi and Wade came into the office for a consultation. To the family's dismay, Wade has been laid off his job. He's been with the company for nearly 25 years, but it didn't guarantee job security. The family lived within their means, took yearly family vacations and put away the bare minimum into an online high yield savings account. However, they dipped into the savings account every year to use as spending money for the elaborate vacation spots. They boasted about the exotic spots such as Italy, France, Greece, Spain, Caribbean Islands, etc.

The couple never discussed how much was enough to put away for emergency funds. They were just excited to brag about having funds in the account. After reviewing statements and comparing to wages, Heidi and Wade only saved three months gross pay. During this recession and possibly worst economic time since the depression, three months isn't adequate.

I suggest saving a year's worth of gross salary. This may sound extreme, but loss of wages (employment) isn't foreseen. This couple didn't prepare for a job loss. Now their two income household is one. Let's also keep in mind that Heidi should be supportive of Wade as he seeks supplemental income. Losing a job is detrimental to one's esteem and emotions.

In the case of Heidi and Wade, they could've easily saved a years income if they put away a percentage and gradually increased. The couple lived within their means, but it wasn't modest. They are big fans of buying designer coffee and eating out for lunch. After reviewing their receipts, it's known they could've collectively saved $275.00 weekly.

I challenge each of you reading the book to find a behavior in your life you can eliminate such as purchasing morning coffee, purchasing a lunch, or buying daily donuts. Whatever your vice attempt to eliminate for one month to notice the increase in savings. During this time of economic crisis, I suggest for everyone to monitor your spending habits.

****

Financial Education

****

Establishing and Maintaining Credit

How do I build my credit to report to the credit bureaus?

Joe Wise spend only what he needed. He
owned two credit cards with modest limits
and established a sound relationship with the
companies. One day Joe was invited to a
birthday party. He knew the party would consist
of the elite who wore the latest designs and lived
without a budget. Against his better judgment,
Joe accepted the offer. He knew he needed a
date to accompany to the party so he contacted
his friend, Pam Shopper. Pam was a co-worker
that always looks great and knew the designers.

She was obsessed with Fashion Week and
emulated every style without regard to cost.
Pam discussed with Joe the attire expected
during the party and all the details the event
consist of. Although, she was accompanying
Joe as a date and never met the birthday girl;
she was compelled to purchase a gift. Pam
was excited and wanted to start looking for a
dress for herself and an unforgettable gift.

"When are we going shopping together? I want
to make sure I have enough money." Yelled Pam.

"Calm down! Since the party is
tomorrow we can go after work if
that's okay with you." Smiled Joe.

"That's fine. I guess I can manage by
rearranging a bill or two before it's due."

That evening Joe and Pam went shopping. The
evening started very slow for Joe because he
was window-shopping while Pam picked up
nearly every item she saw. He had never seen
a person walk around with so much money.
She paid cash for everything. The time came
for them both to go inside a boutique. The
boutique consisted of both men and women
clothing. It was top of the line with vintage
items. Pam immediately spotted a vintage
Prada dress and Joe saw a Dolce & Gabbanna
suit. The dress would take every penny she
had left in her pocket book. Joe evaluated
his funds and thought about the cost. He
wanted to make sure he would be able to
wear the suit again on several occasions.

"Why do you look like you're deep
in thought?" asked Pam

"I'm thinking about how I'm going to pay
for the suit. I don't want to pay for this suit
for the next thirty years." Answered Joe.

"Nothing beats cash!" laughed Pam.

"I know, but I occasionally use a credit card
to help build my credit." Stated Joe.

Pam didn't quite understand why anyone would
use a credit card. She was always told that it
would get a person in trouble. On the contrary,
if used wisely it can help build a person's
credit. Joe was wise enough to only charge fifty
percent of his credit limit and pay the minimum
payment in full or the balance each month.

He was proud of establishing good credit and
had the knowledge to maintain its good standing.
He only held two credit cards one from his
early college days. Although the interest was
extremely higher than he appreciated he didn't
want to close out the history due to a possible
FICO score drop. Joe decided to purchase
the suit with a credit card instead of writing
a check. Since he knew he had the money he
would pay off the balance with the money from
his "leisure funds" as he name the expense
account for outside household purchases. Pam
remaining funds in her pocket was lint and cab
money. She was forced to write a check for the
dress that dipped into her emergency funds.

She believed coming across a vintage dress was an emergency due to possibly being the only one in the room with the dress. Again, Pam loved fashion and fashion loved her monetary dedication. Pam was like many others who believed credits cards were the beginning to an end. She shopped like no other and paid cash. Unbeknownst to her actions it could actually help build credit to one day be able to be offered lowest interest rates and look upon as a Tier A-1 customer.

Joe Wise was conscious of his spending habits. He knew from early on the key steps to establishing and maintaining credit. Joe didn't charge more that fifty percent of the card's credit limit. He makes his payments in full or the minimum payment. Joe Wise follows the recommended steps to credit management. Credit management is needed in order to establish good credit. Credit scores range from 350-850.

The lower the FICO score, the more interest a customer pays. The common goal is to get to a good credit score. There are steps that should be taken into consideration in order to reach the optimal score.

1.   Payment history

2.   Amounts owed (outstanding debt)

3.   Length of credit history

4.   New credit-recently opened accounts, frequency of derogatory credit information (bankruptcies, charge-offs, and collections)

5.   Types of credit used

Individuals noting what it takes to build
and maintain credit are conscious of what
creditors regard when issuing interest.
We are all *wise* individuals and capable
of making smart decisions. However,
education plays an intricate role in furthering
advances toward financial independence.

For those of you whom don't regard the
behaviors it takes to increase a FICO score think
about what makes you charge your purchases
near or beyond the credit limit. Remember
Joe Wise, he was conscious about his spending
habits. He calmly thought about his item,
how he would purchase, and the payoff.

Pam Shopper was a compulsive shopper and purchased using cash. Don't get me wrong I don't think there's anything wrong with cash. However, it should be treated like anything else…use in moderation. Cash should be accessible for small purchases and on hand emergency funds. She had the wrong misconception about credit cards just as many of you do. Credit is why the economy is in its current state. With that being said we need *positive* credit. Start with a low credit limit card to use wisely. Purchase small denomination items and either pay the balance or the minimum payment. Pam is a great example of how a person can establish a leisure account by setting money in an account from each paycheck. Once she decides to shop she can spend no more than fifty percent of the credit limit and no more than what is established in the account.

Think about a time when you purchased items
and how you felt during that moment.

EMOTIONAL FINANCIAL CHART

(Take the time to think)

NAME THE ITEM PURCHASED

1.

2.

3.

WHAT WERE YOUR FEELINGS?

1.

2

3.

As you look at the purchases in the chart and the emotions, you encountered at the time it's clear to note that *Finances are linked to Emotions.*

Deposit Accounts

How do I begin to establish a relationship with a financial institution?

Interacting with numerous people involves answering questions from credit to investments. To begin, establishing a relationship whether financial or partners involves proper selection, patience, and inquiring about satisfaction of needs. There are more financial institutions than a consumer can bear. Once you decide which one suits your needs then it's time to establish a relationship. I suggest starting simple then taking advantage of all your account offers.

Deposit accounts are the beginning to a
lasting relationship. It can initiate the
discipline needed to move forward in the
financial world. Begin by properly saving
and seeking accounts that can keep up with
inflation. I have consulted with clients who
have the (depression baby) syndrome.

*Mr. Jones refuses to open an account. He
rather pays a fee to negotiate a check. Mr.
Jones pay for everything cash and has never
established credit for himself. He has horrific
stories of the depression and remembers when
his parents could not afford to buy soap and
lard. Many representatives have sat down
with Mr. Jones to discuss the benefits of an
account, but he never wants to hear it.*

Will he ever change his mind?

Mr. Jones has neglectful, abandoned emotions toward deposit accounts. His establishment toward a lasting relationship with financial institutions consists of his parents' turmoil of not making ends meet and hearing stories of lost monies.

The days of uninsured monies have been at ease with FDIC products. Again, deposit accounts can help accomplish financial goals. Maintain good standing and continue to build with small personal loans and credit cards. Nowadays, banks are starting to be a one stop need for customers.

Budget and Managing

Is it possible to live within my means?

Absolutely! One day I was eating lunch with family. I overheard a conversation because the restaurant is a cozy setting. The group of friends was deciding to go Dutch and one person disclosed he didn't have much cash. However, he ordered the most from the menu. When the bill arrived, he pulled out a credit card, smiled and said, "go big or go home".

When you carefully monitor what accessible cash you have on hand, it is possible to live within your means. We have become a credit society. I am not opposing to establishing credit; it's maintaining that we overlook.

To survive within your means there are
essentials for finances are linked to emotions:

1. Set a budget

Establishing a budget for whatever your needs is
essential when living within your means. I was
watching a show on Bravo TV and heard someone
indicate she didn't have a budget. The spending
was ridiculous! If you have it to spare of course
"treat yourself". However, even the wealthiest
have lost millions. The worst thing anyone can
do is continuously spend without regard to what
you actually have. The well informed spender
is prepared and looks at the tag for cost.

2. Set goals

Set a goal! Set a goal! Regardless of short term or
long term goals allow you to stay on path. The first
thing I ask a client during a consultation is what you
like to accomplish and in what timeframe. A well
written plan is indicative of staying within a budget as
well as paying off bills expeditiously. I believe goals
should also be established outside a financial setting.

3. Identify spending triggers

Take a moment to reflect what triggers you to spend
money. Is it loneliness? Is it wanting to be the first
to wear an original? Is it happiness? Identifying
what your triggers are will allow you to address
your spending habits. When I meet with various
clients I notice a correlation between an emotion and
outlandish spending. Take a moment to write down
precipitating events before going on a shopping spree.

4. Surround self with supporters

Surrounding yourself with individuals that have a common goal is essential to living within your means. As with any relationship people have to have the same values in order to have a successful relationship. When you verbally disclose what your intentions are with your group of friends it is beneficial for everyone to respect and implement.

5. Educate about finances

Reading is fun as well as fundamental. You can never subscribe to or read too many books about financial education. I recommend everyone begin by journaling daily about your spending habits and the various emotions you possibly identify when triggered. The world is consumed with an abundance of information that is easily accessible. The internet is a beginning to acquiring documentation that is less economical or free.

6. Set boundaries

The boundaries are set with you when a budget is
established. However, this particular boundary is
recognized for others who plead for monies and
request for loans. As I have coached clients in the
past to look into the mirror and practice saying, "No"!
Recently, a mother came into the office distressed
the nearly six figure savings has depleted to less than
$3000.00. She hadn't realized that she was spending
that much money on others. She disclosed her only
son who is an engineer lost his job. He is married
with two children. The wife is a homemaker who has
no desire to change her job title. I encouraged her to
cut the cord and persuade him to find employment
any if it involved relocating. She is the typical
parent who put others' needs before hers. It's time
to say No or you'll financially spiral downward.

7. Love self

Although, each essential listed is highly recommended
for achievement. Loving yourself is going to be
indicative to a successful plan. Put your needs
first and identify what truly makes you happy.
Self is key to the cognitive representation of
one's identity. In order to progress in personal
management it's imperative to acknowledge one's
shortcomings and establish realistic future goals.

Implementing these steps is imperative to living
within your means and establishing wealth
for yourself. Remember, anyone is capable
of getting out of debt. It's identifying the
cause that is affecting the continuous behavior.
Before acknowledging, the fundamental
steps to living within a budget address the
debt. It is essential to know where you stand
in your financial dilemma. Be aware of
your total balances, payments and rates.

****

Letters of Concern

****

Dear Bahiyah Shabazz:

I have been in financial turmoil for quite some time. I am
capable of making ends meet, but not enough to enjoy
occasional vacationing. I have spoken to my friends
about my financial dilemma and they encourage me to
file bankruptcy. I have played with the thought, but I
honestly believe I can eradicate my bills without doing so.

Since the end of the year is approaching I am concerned
about listing a resolution. I want to get out of debt,
but it is easier said than done. What steps should
I take and should I consider filing bankruptcy?

Sincerely,

Stacy Miller

Dear Stacy,

Thanks for the letter. Many people are in your predicament. I don't believe you should file for bankruptcy. I have noticed that too many people are using bankruptcy as a scapegoat to starting over. Having a few delinquent bills doesn't constitute a consultation from an attorney. It may only involve reevaluation of your spending habits. You indicated that you are able to make ends meet. Your only situation is not being able to take vacations. This is the least of your problems. Unfortunately, that is a small price to pay when you are throwing money away.

I suggest you write down every item you purchase for the next three weeks. You would be amazed at the amount of money you are spending on "important" items. Next, create a budget and set reasonable timeline goals. This will assist in accomplishing your financial resolution. Lastly, look into a debt reduction plan and apply extra funds toward monthly bills to get out of debt sooner.

Sincerely,

Bahiyah Shabazz

Personal Management Consultant

Shabazz Management Group, LLC

Greetings Ms. Shabazz,

I purchased a home nearly three years ago and to my dismay the payments have increased. I was extremely excited to qualify that I didn't read the terms. After the second year my monthly payment doubled. I contacted the Mortgage Company to complain, but I was informed the contract had an adjustable rate.

I'm not able to make ends meet and have missed two consecutive payments. Recently, I came across a kind individual who offered to purchase the home from me. I am seriously contemplating selling the house. However, don't I have to have the house on the market before I can proceed?

I am exhausted about my financial situation. Each time I turn on the television I hear about more homes going into foreclosure. I don't want to be added to the list of statistics. Can you please help?

Thank you,

Marcia Thompson

Dear Marcia,

Thanks for the letter. During this economic turmoil many people are falling prey to the foreclosure crisis. It is extremely important that you read all terms of a contract. I know it is very exciting being a first time home owner, but it is your responsibility to read each line. Remember, at this point the ball is in your hands. The title company has no choice but to be patient and answer all questions.

I recommend you take the kind man's offer. It is truly lucky for you to find someone to take the house off your hands. You don't even have to have the house on the market to do so. I suggest you catch up on the payments as best as possible. He can then refinance the house into his name. Selling the house before it reaches foreclosure will help your credit.

Sincerely,

Bahiyah Shabazz

Personal Management Consultant

Shabazz Management Group, LLC

Dear Ms. Shabazz:

I am a recent college graduate who is seeking employment.
I have a Bachelors of Science in Business Administration.
I want to continue my education and earn a Doctorate.
However, I now have $32000.00 in college tuition that
I owe. In addition, I am seeking employment, but I am
unsure of what field I should pursue. I didn't realize
there is so much opportunity with a social degree.

I am confused about my future. Should I put
off my goal of earning a doctorate and focus
on employment to pay off the tuition?

Sincerely,

Jennifer Johnson

Dear Jennifer,

Thanks for the letter. Let me begin by congratulating you on your accomplishment. Education is extremely important and you have embraced that belief. Why do you believe you have to earn either a doctorate or work? It is possible to perform both tasks if you are capable of doing so.

I am open to many opportunities. I suggest you set your goals, prioritize and review daily as a reminder. First, seek employment that will allow you to grow after earning a doctorate. Next, inquire about tuition reimbursement. If you find employment that has tuition reimbursement you don't have to worry about financing your doctorate program.

There are many people seeking online education. This nontraditional setting allows you to work at your own pace. You can defer paying back your tuition as long as you are enrolled in college. I suggest you do pay at least the interest payments on your undergraduate bill so that it doesn't revolve. Too many times graduates neglect to read the terms of deferment to realize the principal has increased year over year.

Sincerely,

Bahiyah Shabazz

Personal Management Consultant

Shabazz Management Group, LLC

Attn: Shabazz Management Group

I understand how important it is to establish an emergency
fund. I don't know where to start. I like to spend my
money on beer, chips and chicks. I am always told by
a parent that now is the right time because I am still
young. As a 23-year-old guy I think I have enough time.

I own a condominium, have a great job and earn more
than my friends earn. Should I wait until I'm out of my
partying stage? I have enough time to save money. My
parents are concerned about my spending habits.

Thank you,

Matt O'Brian

Dear Matt,

It's nice to hear you are enjoying your life. It sounds like you are the life of the party amongst your friends. I don't want to deter you from enjoying your life because you are clearly doing that. When life becomes mundane, it becomes uninteresting.

This is a great time to start an emergency fund. The ideal amount is a year salary. Start with a financial plan to see how much you need to put away during paychecks. Open a high yield savings account that will maximize your interest opportunity.

Sincerely,

Bahiyah Shabazz

Personal Management Consultant

Shabazz Management Group, LLC

****

Belief In Success

****

To succeed we must first believe that we can.
~Anonymous

Remember the three R's: Respect
for self, Respect for others and
Responsibility for all your actions

Our emotional wholeness is committed
from within. We have a tendency to express
ourselves through many venues. Rather it's
shopping, working, reading, volunteering or
spiritual. We have a responsibility to lead
and respect others and ourselves. Many
times people notice themselves in a rut
and subconsciously refuse to move on. In
order to receive an emotional and spiritual
blessing, release the negativity surrounding.

Identify your triggers that allow you to
spend. Address your concerns and surround
yourself with a firm, supportive, happy
group of friends. Regarding the respect
they have for themselves will allow you
to take responsibility for your actions and
treat others, as you want to be treated.

You are a beautiful person that can and will
take control of your finances. Let today
be the first day of your life. Erase all the
negativity you have about your financial
settings and start to educate yourself.

Respect for self

Respect for self comes in many different forms. It's respect for your body, beliefs, morals, values and finances. It is undue justice when you make a conscious effort to uphold your values and neglect your finances. How you actively engage in your finances states a lot about you. Think of your household as a small business and you are the CEO/CFO. The company can't sufficiently run without your executive decisions and financial guidance. You have to regard your financial statements to balance your books. Make sure you completely understand that each move and decision affects the company's financial outcome.

Begin each day with an affirmation. Journal your daily thoughts to regard what trigger you emotionally and write down what you spend for the day. Embrace yourself and admire who you are. Remember, you are capable of demanding respect from yourself.

Financial responsibility begins with self.

Respect for others

Respect others as well as yourself. When
you are involved with a group of friends
it is ideal for all of you to have common
goals. Again, regard how others treat
themselves and uphold their beliefs. One
of the worst things you can do is disregard,
abuse your financial status and overstep your
boundaries with others. I have noticed more
than often when people outlandishly spend
their monies they ask others for theirs.

The playground rule of sharing doesn't apply
to this life's lesson. Don't get me wrong
sharing *is* caring. Nevertheless, care enough
about yourself not to involve others in your
financial dilemma. Don't look for anyone
to bail you out of your financial situation.

Success begins with your contribution
to society. One person didn't create the
economic crisis we are currently involved. It
was a collective action from everyone.

Responsibility for all your actions

Don't blame others for what has happened in
your life. You are the pilot of your ship. Sure
enough things happen in our lives that we don't
have control over. It is what you learn from
that life lesson and apply going forward that
matters. Again, state your goals, prioritize and
accomplish. When a setback occurs reevaluate
your goals to accommodate the situation.

Demanding respect for yourself and
identifying the emotional state you're in at
times is indicative of your actions. Live, act
and become successful in all facets of your
life. When you are consumed with positive
thoughts and beliefs there isn't anything you
can't do once you put your mind to it.

Define who you are...

There is so much in a name. It's
also important how it is said.

Hi, my name is Bahiyah Shabazz. I am a
personal management consultant. Whomever
you are be proud of yourself and yell what
you stand for. Morals, values, beliefs
and representation define who you are.
Embrace yourself and represent well!
Remember the old cliché, "If you fall for
anything, you'll stand for nothing".

What do you stand for? How do
you want others to see you?

I want to be seen as successful and adequate.
In order to be viewed in that light it's
extremely important that is what I present.

I came across a woman who defined herself
by her group of friends. All were successful
in their careers and had no problem with
introduction. Each wore elaborate clothing,
lived in dream homes, drove luxury cars, and
vacation. Most importantly, Tiffany explained
that she believed they all lived within their
means. None of them had a problem with
saying when. She on the hand defined herself
by *their* successes. She was the chameleon
amongst the friends and everyone knew it. The
group of women knew that Tiffany would adjust
herself to conform to anyone personality.

She never took the time out to establish her
personality. The group of women would
actually benefit from a balance setting. Again,
surrounding yourself with friends that have
a common goal consists of happiness. I
encouraged Tiffany to take some time out for
herself. She admired the women so much
that she lost herself amongst her friends.

Begin with tapping into your soul and listening
to your heart. Journal each moment.

You are beautiful no matter what they say.
Words can't get you down.
                    ~Christiana Aguilerra

Am I good enough for....?

Self doubt is harmful and can deter you
from reaching your goals. The first step to
success is acknowledgment. Believe that you
control your destiny. Never consider other's
negative perception of you. When you fall
prey to the judgment of others you become
vulnerable and begin to question yourself.

Absolutely! You are good enough for anyone
and anything. Excellence takes practice. Initiate
your day with an affirmation, create a list of
goals and stay positive. Your attitude must
remain optimistic to attract upbeat thoughts.

Respect yourself and others will respect you.
Your statute will insist others to believe that you
are good enough for whatever you present.

Live up to your expectations not others

Don't define yourself by what others
think of you. When you begin to define
yourself by others perception then you are
caught in their beliefs and not of yours.

Remembering to respect yourself, defining
who you are, and realizing you are good
enough for whatever you set your mind to is
imperative for success. Set limitations as to
what you are willing to accept from others
and what you are devoted to portraying.

Reflections, Thoughts & Notes

Reflection, Thoughts & Notes

About the Author

Bahiyah Shabazz grew up always knowing she would help others. Her educational path allowed her the expertise she currently uses. With a psychology and financial background, Bahiyah noticed how society recklessly spends money. The outlandish spending derives from emotional spending, which she felt must be addressed.

Bahiyah Shabazz is the CEO of Shabazz Management Group, LLC. She is a personal management consultant and motivational speaker. She holds a B.A. in Psychology and Minority Studies and M.B.A. concentrating in Finance. For many years, she has worked in the financial industry.

Bahiyah Shabazz is noted as a prolific writer who captivates audiences, takes a therapeutic approach to finances and encourages others to get in touch with self.

For more information about Bahiyah Shabazz, go to bahiyahshabazz.com or email at smg_inquiry@bahiyahshabazz.com

For weekly blogs visit: bahiyahshabazz.blogspot.com

Contact Information:
Shabazz Management Group, LLC
PO Box 14041
Merrillville, In. 46411
219-588-6113